the stargazers

the stargazers

JAMES MCKEE

atmosphere press

Table of Contents

to Annie
sine te, nihil

Domesticated

You've never built a house.
So in raising these walls, you just
bank them round like a nest
with stray chipped bricks you found.

Then for title to that house,
you trench a line around it
and withdraw, crisply bounded,
to such peace as your moods allow.

Some nights you pace your house
behind shut blinds, and cheer
where decay or disrepair
preview its tumbling down;

come dawn, no grander houses
ask your keeping, so you rise
to paint and plaster and reglaze:
nothing here for neighbors to doubt.

From the crates its crawlspaces house
in a brooding closeness, these rooms
draw a force to hold, like a home's.
Even the view belongs to you now.

The Death of Gaddafi

You've seen the video: a blur of limbs in beige
    and olive; a desert hillscape; glimpses of a red
something; male faces wrung with triumph or rage;
    the camera-ringed convergence by a pickup's bed.

It's him: that skidmark moustache, those gunslit eyes.
    The flabby stasis surgeries have stuccoed to his face
shows garishly unyouthful, though it does disguise
    frailties that might have cut short his disgrace.

Watch once more as, hustled towards us by a dozen hands,
    he fingers the blood raying out from his temple,
recoils from it, as if now he understands,
    and suddenly sits in the dust when his legs crumple.

Is he begging? threatening? Only the *takbir* is audible.
    He cannot know how few minutes more he has
till zoomed-in, slow-motion footage becomes uploadable
    of a dazed, wild-haired old man getting knifed in the ass.

Once resplendent in the plunder of his long reign,
    now just a poor, bare animal, soon to die;
though Gaddafi cannot pay all he owes in pain,
    you think it only just to watch him try.

It happens off-camera. He's dead when you see him again.
    While his stripped corpse proves his own shame is finished,
such a power to implicate is given some men
    that even in their riddance are we diminished.

Morning Commute with Revenant

i.m. R.M.M.

You know how it is: going in to work,
who looks anything? You're late, it's cold,
hot, raining, no buses *again*, whatever.
You're long past fighting this fast-forward blur,
pure A-to-B time, better numbed than bored.

But then the street views you sluice through slow and lock:
some old warehouse abutting a blacktop lot.
Why here? Don't say a bird.
You do and this is *over.*
No birds, no clouds, nothing with petals or fur.
What then? Don't expect much:
high up this soot-caked chainlink fence
that nets, for no one else, blank swaths of sky,
there juts forth a sawn-off sumac branch,
em dash black and cocked at ten-to-three.

See it first, since you must, as a quenched torch,
a club hanging half-swung,
or someone's bony forearm thrust through the mesh,
lopped at wrist and elbow, and left as a warning.
Fine. But you're not one to confuse
fancied-up musings with the truth:
one hapless stick is all the chainsaw left
the day someone decided
this tree—a weed that wedged upwards from
the crack its seed happened among,
that rose against the traffic-ravaged air,
piercing that fence and knuckling this pavement up—

had to come down.
Rough cobblestones plug the square yard
where its raw stump once weathered anvil-hard;
no doubt the sheared-off roots still grip
deep undertiers of pipe and stone.

A passing siren's wave-crest flushes you
back in the churning surf of city noise,
but by now it's too late:
you've gone and glimpsed that voided silhouette,
you've heard, in its tousling leaves' soundless hiss,
another of those random sidewalk elegies
work alone can dismiss.
And not because it isn't true,
because it is.

Crow

Asked for a favorite bird,
no one says, "Crow,"
nor should it seem strange
this is so.

Plumage like his delivers
little delight
beyond the vandal's thrill
of inked-out light.

Social by nature, he must
roost in mobs,
nesting beside the neighbors
whom he robs.

His colloquies, all crass squawks
and prim clacks,
shock the fluent afresh
with what speech lacks.

His moods, whether raucous, sullen,
giddy or severe,
fool no one who must also
go in fear.

Charmless, too, is his art
of mimicry,
among wits so whetted
to mockery.

But to whom are a crow's joys
not known,
when free to despoil
for sport alone?

Through the Ruins

Your guidebook's tinted overlays
   tidily restore
this palace's lost stories, as you gaze
   on its mosaic floor
      long open to the sky,
      brick walls waist-high.

You stroll the royal avenue
   half-paved with sand,
pocketing odd chunks, as tourists do,
   until at last you stand
      where, from an elbow of stone,
      a tree has grown.

Of the temple or shrine that here once rose,
   nothing is left
but these corner blocks, whose buckling shows
   where a once-minute cleft
      was found by an olive sprout,
      threaded, filled out,

and year by year nudged farther apart
   by the thickening trunk.
Because its sunward rise had to start
   where its roots by chance were sunk,
      it has never ramified free
      of the masonry

that itself owes what shape it keeps
    to one tree's crabbed hold.
(As for the other nearby heaps
    of rubble, they enfold
        no life to anchor them still
        in their builder's will.)

Look how its impacted bark bulges,
    as if squeezed from the seam
joining two stones, trellised by their edges
    to right angles that seem
        the work of circumstance
        more than this plant's.

Yet if, of a form so tortuous,
    the cause is plain,
the same cannot be said for us,
    since the strange ruins that train
        our own balked, oblique climb
        are quarried from time.

Going with the Flow

If flux once locks its theme to things—
the framing exit dream's
self-aware same-bed reawakening,
one abruptly sulfur gingko
the cue for a further August's undoing,
a slow soft rinse of rain
to aid the sidewalk's sloughing
off of chalked-on hopscotch lanes—
good luck dodging the frivolity it brings.
Things end, things end, it says,
it's just what they do.
Oh I know, you reply
smiling at nothing,
me, too.

Trust Me, I've Done This Before

To feel at each step
that fang of glass
lancing deep

through soft sole flesh,
probing for bone
as membranes yield,

stringlets of pain
stitching toes to heel,
and the flinch-faced walk

inflicted by some-
thing somebody broke,
must be to blame

if you of all people
sit still for my scalpel.

Climbing Mount Royal

The rot remains with us, the men are gone.
Derek Walcott

New to the place, I thrust
the blackout drapes apart;
from a suite aiming west
some four centuries up,
my sightlines sweep to a stop
on a hillside's emerald arc.

Montreal's matrix, like sheets
of pentimentoed diagrams,
parquets the earth beneath
except where this green fin
rips through. I thrum right then
like a tuning fork at the summons

struck by those heights. Downstairs,
I can feel the city's hem fraying
as its streets cant up steeply,
till a last curbstone frontiers
what, with a shrug, my maps supply
no paths for, bluntly daring

me to enter. So I enter.
Encroached on by oaks and maples
that seem stricken with some stark question,
I must parry with selfies and labels.
Gouged-through switchbacks lever
me upward as smoothly as when,

a child, I could sleep through long
rancorous car rides home
as if still uncompromised. . . . The woods
admit the vista in shreds,
its perpendiculars jarringly plumb,
till I reach this plaza slung

out from the crest, and behold
at last how the St. Lawrence runs
like a gash, stitched with bridgemetal,
across tar and cement accretions.
Where the downslope flats, a stand
of towers smokestacks level

with this terrace, my po-mo hotel
among them. There, I thought here
quaint and vestigial, not this shrine
to a Cartier still gallant behind
his fleur-de-lys and crucifix, still
grappling these horizons as far

as now to his New France.
What it takes to get a man plinthed
I know from home, where our myths
rear up real as monuments
that brood, like scarecrows of bronze,
over fields fructified by wrongs.

It's time to go. Descent
restores nothing but distance
to what whispers, even through glass,
of the first, the lost, and the last,
of the all gone, of the soon going,
and of that world, the new one, now coming.

Urban Life

I've got all the nature I need, here in the city.
 Blocks of green speckle its grid where parks and zoos
nestle like pets, cosseted and car-ad pretty,
while vermin and weeds, too close to us for pity,
 adapt to every toxin we dare to use.

The one time I went, the Orchid Show was as hot
 and human-humid as the subway. I had to leave.
In its crowd, each splayed plant dangled from a pot
as if petaling just to please us, which it was not.
 Out where the traffic sang through the streets, I could breathe.

Crews plant trees now with a bark said to repel
 pollution, which I call progress since whatever
kills them is plainly killing us as well.
Down my block, saplings stand yoked between parallel
 uprights, the better for breaking them to our weather.

I saw a hummingbird last week, which was weird:
 a hovering emerald, exotic even for Queens.
Something like joy rayed through me, only to disappear
since wherever its wing-blur belonged, it wasn't here.
 I try, but cannot not know what it meant. Means.

The Donkeys of Petra

I

Boldly through sand and scree and sightseers ride
the Bedouin: their splendid robes flaring wide,
boot-heels skimming the ground,
eyes fiercely kohled,
while the rods they hold
land with a bracing sound
on the rumps of the small flop-eared donkeys they sit astride.

2

Up where the ancient rock-cut stairways twine
past charred cave tombs toward a long-unhonored shrine,
they ferry one load more
to the mesa's top
without a stop,
then descend to the valley floor
to spare fresh riders the punishment of such a climb.

3

Tourists, their logoed outerwear tinted with dust
in the desert sandstone's palette of brick and rust,
indecorously straddle
their rented mounts,
taming their doubts
with bit and goad and saddle,
as all who would master these willful beasts surely must.

4

I too once rode. Aged nine, unbroken still
to my own burdens, I beat my animal
       into a headlong trot
           jolting enough
           to fling me off
     for good. I never forgot
scurrying like a bug under the hoofs whose kicks could kill.

5

Yet since that donkey patiently looked away
from my struggle to right myself, I walk today,
       passing each muleteer
           like a man blind
           to his own kind,
     who cannot help but hear
a reproach in every unanswerable, urgent, put-upon bray.

The Road to Lake Avernus

                                                    runs, ha-ha, unlit.
Just rumpled blacktop ribboning plumb-straight
under oaks ranked close as rungs.
                                  Which we drive in rain,
cold rain, loose fistfuls of shot flung
across our windshield. Some sheds look away.
                                            Why'd we come?
A sign we saw, a turn we took, a whim
we just went with, and at the worst time to visit
anything ever. Unless it's the best.

Sulphurous waters said to kill birds mid-
flight'd seemed, this morning, far too *meh* for docked
winter sunlight,
                            though not for a night like this.
Parked and profane, we find our "entrance to Hades"
sprinkled with gulls and ducks. *Black* ducks,
get it? Sure: *Aeneid* Book V. Make that VI,
as confirmed by Google.
                              So the mood's as it should be
when the hard-faced *padrone* of a shoreside café
eye-rakes us, shrugs, and resumes his pink
Gazzetta dello Sport. Another look
out at black waves, while I wondered (did you?)
at our crisp dismissal. How'd he know?
                                      We go,
saying we'll come back when there's sun. Which we won't.

Our cold Fiat warms. Let's find someplace to eat.
Time now for tomorrow-talk, for maps and money, as
raindrops, swarming like ions, flare through our highbeams.

A Change of Sky

> *caelum non animum mutant qui trans*
> *mare currunt* (To travel across the sea
> brings a change of sky, not of soul)
>   Horace

Bystander-slack, all aplomb and delicious exemption,
I'm a benchful of pricey sprawl outside the kibbutz hotel,
awaiting the bus to Masada, made capital-g glorious by mass
          suicide in 73 CE.
Far down a slope of drone-prowled sand scabbed with outcrops,
          a sea—
yes, the Dead one—
flares back at the sky like a sheet of pitted steel.
Turns out I *like* my vistas cleansed enough for, say,
phylacteried zealots and phalanxed legionaries to suffer just as
          superbly
as a good-kitschy network miniseries, *circa* 1980, could imagine
          them.
It's simpler that way, like not listening.
Meantime, shadows creep like wet ink beneath olive-drab scrub
while a hot hush, as between blows,
clots in the burdened air.

All at once I un-slump: across the road stands an ibex, too real to
          be random,
horns like flourished sabers, outthrust pharaoh's beard, hoofs of
          battered onyx.
It surveys the façade, side-eyes me curtly, then clops over the hot
          frontier—
if driveways count as frontiers—
and in among pool-blockading and palm-surveilled bungalows
          planted

where olive trees and flocks of sheep once belonged
to people who don't belong here anymore.
I look around: no one to witness it step through that rent in the
          probable
which has, like *that,*
zipped shut behind its quickening trot.

Whatever it is I feel stands me up, god *damn* it,
fierce as a prophet for a good scourging by some truths:
mass immiseration, a carceral shadow-state,
dark-age atavisms thickly nacred in digital frivolity,
the whole hypertrophied apparatus of a wartime imperium
still lubricated by its founding crimes, but soon—
too soon—
I hear the heave and grind of my bus lurching up the
          switchbacks.
Any minute now, the doors will open with a hiss and a clunk,
a gush of air conditioning and Mid-Atlantic English will blur the
          desert glare,
and in a candy-hued touchscreen glow that soothes like home
I'll sit where the look no one gives me proves I still belong.

At the Frick

I: 1919

Midnight. The city's uproar has paused at last.
Gas flames dance as he shuffles by.
The cache of masterworks he has amassed
wait, to amuse and edify.

His parlor. Saint Jerome's eyes search the drift
of shadows and ropy cigar smoke.
Saint Francis, too, suffers the seraph's gift.
The War was lost without his coke.

One axe for More and Cromwell. What will they say?
The fortune first, followed by the "crimes,"
then just his paintings. "Left by Henry Clay
Frick, the works offer future times

the truest portrait of the man himself." What years
and wealth fail to efface, art will.
Velazquez. Rembrandt. Hals. His three Vermeers
alone show off the matchless skill

of their collector. "My West Gallery
is worth a hundred Homesteads. Look
at this Corot, that Turner, and say of me
I always paid for what I took."

II: 2020

"...To Goya's *Forge*, a late work, Mr. Frick's
frequent nighttime visits are well known.
Note how the open brushstrokes deftly fix
the opposing forces of steel and bone. . . ."

The docent gestures toward the backstage gloom
in which this humble trio toils,
then sweeps her charges into a further room
hung with gilt-framed baronial spoils.

While the rest, once a haremed stock of wives,
recall their owner's gaze no more,
this austere smithy artfully contrives
to hold its ex-proprietor.

One pumps the bellows, one clamps the tongs tight,
a third swings a blunt sledgehammer high,
forming, in the hot steel's unforgiving light,
a work to damn Frick's memory by.

III: 1919

"Too clean. Ironwork's a soot-blackened trade. . . .
Hah, one that buys landscapes and duchesses!
Once it's a museum, let them stamp my account *paid*.
To him that hath, the Gospel says."

The Warthog

01/20/17

Bowel-born grunts rumble up and out of him
bulking squatly there, paunch-cumbered, plaque-haired,
bludgeon-snout snuffling damply twixt tined tusks.
The mouth pouts till it gets to sneer or bellow.

He stiffens, slackens. From under the rump, lumps
drop softly, disturb not at all his nonchalance
that sewers us, nothings who stare stonestruck on.
At you, maybe, a sludge-tinted eye side-flicks
contempt like acid, scalding now, worse tomorrow.
Take care: at too-long lookers and touch-close crowders,
with out-of-nowhere quickness he'll lunge and gore.
Even the gutted's last gout of blame blames love.

Once oft-snubbed, now alpha, this boar would be feared,
and these days it's his zoo we back-forth through, his
slop we guzzle, his whelps we coddle and long
to wallop. Go ahead: be abased. Abashed.
Abandoned, even. Gorge on rage. Rebrand hate
as a duty. Perorate. Plot. Only this:

The numbed grip nothing. Instead, bear your shame, stab-sharp,
against all piggery in the long pig-days to come.

Departure

Like escaping through a siege, growing older
    hampers itself with hopes of return;
so if, over your bare shoulder,
upwind palaces start to smolder,
    let them burn.

Woken by ax-hack and sword-clang, at once you knew
    better than to arm for the defense
of gates your foes stream through.
You're free to act as the conquered do
    when a war ends.

Whatever you cannot bear, you must jettison
    to gain the stealth of lacking a past.
You're not safe till you outrun
hearing the hoard of spoils you've won
    unamassed.

Shrieks. Towers crash down. Yet back-alleying
    at a pace fit for fifty, not twenty,
you must curb the urge to cling
a moment to some random one or thing,
    from the passing plenty.

Beyond the walls, your descent shoreward lies
    through olive groves long since laid waste.
Dawn miscolors smoke-splashed skies,
leaving you no shield against hunting eyes
    but further haste.

What exiles converge on this fringe of wrack-strewn sand?
    What refuge beckons from this blank sea?
Comes there no one to command
our foretold voyage to a land
    called Italy?

In the Ruins of a Tyrant's Palace

I.
   Leering like some grim old satyr, the porter
sallies from his lodge's nicotine-ochre fug
to intercept your sauntering-by. *Now money.
No map. Close soon.* Paid, he resumes his morning
gameshows and *grappa*, while that blotched, forbidding face
lingers like the film (or was it TV?) avatar
of him who built this pile and at whose death
it burned, to endure sullenly as plundered hulk,
quarry for drystone, midden, picturesque view and,
these days, attraction.

2.
     Sinkpipe guardrails, crudely
cemented-in, narrowly sluice tourists through
a fractured arch, past doorways agape to the sky
or gagged with rubble, around a lichenous portico
caging a fountain's rust-caked stump, then through
to a vast bare hall where, beneath its then-unpunctured
roof, favorites preened in the fierce mood-field emitted
from its daised far end. Sunbeams drop and scatter
like shrapnel across bald pavingstones asizzle
in the dust of your passing. Off dank corridors, notched
with a pantheon of purged niches, room implicates room,
husked of all residue but his: blasphemous rants
scudding the bowed heads of trembling nobles, rituals
bizarre and defiling, annihilations roughed out
over maps noded like synapses. From this wrecked terrace
fatuous whims flurried forth to harry the wits
of a war-sick people; down these walls, continents
voided their curses like filthy pelting rain.

3.
In a poem,

the rustle of crumbling tile might summon a hush
as at his approach; the kite's muffled caw, a flinch
as at the scrape of his grindstone voice. But you know
you know better. So scavenge a chunk of brick
for your desk, then pause for a last look over the cliff
whence were hurled,

        shrieking,

            those who displeased. Up here,
the cadence of waves creaming against the rocks
measures another tide unheard, and the white,
chevron-winged seabirds wheel and sweep for their prey
through the soundlessness of distance, as sundering as that
of fear.

Nothing to Do Now but Wait

Late March, and still
brightest days chill,
   while cloud-roofed freeze;
sunshine cedes cold
unslackened hold
   over bare trees.

One thaw ago,
ramparts of snow
   stood sternly massed;
their breadth and height,
each week less white,
   seemed sure to last.

Gone they may be
entirely
   from lot and street,
yet, like black rust,
thick salt-scabs crust
   the cracked concrete.

Hulking and gray,
blocks stretch away
   in frost-bleached rows;
where pavement ice
catches the eyes,
   a hard sky shows.

The year's routine
is stalled, between
    what has not started,
and what, as though
forever so,
    has not departed.

Change must soon come.
With winter done,
    on each dark bough
green fuzz will form
as winds grow warm.
    Soon. But not now.

All Before Them

One day, Adam gave Eve a look.
"What now?" "Up for a walk?" "No. Where?"
"You know where," Adam said. "Bad idea."
He stared. She sighed. The path they took
was one not used since their exile here.

"Hello there," the Cherub said.
"It's been a while. You'll need to leave."
"Hold on," said Adam. "Let's go," said Eve.
"We know we're banned. We didn't forget,"
Adam said. "Just a quick look. Please."

The Cherub shrugged, "Watch out for the Sword,"
and stood aside. There was the Gate,
towering, austere, and firmly chained.
Adam listened for some sign of God;
Eve missed feeling unashamed.

Yet beyond its bars, the landscape was more
or less the same as that outside.
They gazed where low hills hid the sight
of orchards once theirs to tend, which bore
fruits not tasted since their flight.

"Time's up," came the Cherub's voice.
So, not looking at one another
and in silence, they returned together
to their fields, their hut, and their two boys,
who had never known their parents so tender.

Pilgrimage

Visiting your childhood home
half a continent away,
we are left by chance alone,
family crush at bay.

As we savor this brief lull,
girding ourselves to resume
stations in the crucible
of that crowded room,

you repeat a nursery rhyme
treasured since you were a girl,
which had lodged one sand-speck line
where it was to pearl:

"Thursday's child has far to go"—
noise floods through an opening door—
then you add, standing to go,
"I was made for more."

So you were. I trailed you in,
like a pilgrim come to trace
where the footsteps would begin,
leading from this place.

Leaving the Anne Frank House

After the fraught hush beyond the secret door,
it comes as a relief
to sit through the uplift of this epilogue film,
collecting yourself to leave.

Upstairs, though you knew the story, you'd been ambushed
by her bedroom, so bare and small,
the tourists abruptly mute, and the Garbo stills
she had pasted to the wall.

But now, in this bright, glass-walled space, you watch
while a dozen interviews
attest to the hope found here, humble yet potent
as the acorns an oak-tree strews.

On then to the gift-shop, where merchandise
will do its part to assuage
your taut lurching between flayed tenderness
and sullen, outletless rage.

Yet would it not be better, somehow, to pass
straight from house to street
and prowl, aggrieved and unappeasable,
through the Amsterdammers you meet?

This bearded sophisticate looks like a fascist,
that fit young mom, an informer;
bystanders and bad Samaritans bike past
a quisling on the corner.

Evil winters within us like a fat black bulb
some bad spring will split wide
to add its blossom to history's horror garden—
Exactly what Anne denied.

Talking Past Each Other

This was promised in our stars
Nothing taught you trust like force
These are ours and that is yours
Talking only makes it worse

> Whatever you take from us, you soon leave gutted
> hacking away the whorls our dead palms printed.

God's own sword can work no crime
You were shiftless till we came
Do not step across that line
We still mispronounce your names

> Like flesh chewing on a lodged arrow's barbs,
> your memories callus tightly around our loss.

All we mean you contradict
Like claims like and that's a fact
One look at you makes us sick
Get out now and don't come back

> Our riddance still promises you peace, as if
> the goad of your fierce unrest were not our grief.

The Exes

Once more, my love,
let us two take
the measure of
each one's mistake.

Yours was an ass
who hoped a string
of sneers could pass
for husbanding.

Mine generated
so much shrill drama,
she incarnated
some vengeful karma.

To yours, a wife
must know she is
fortunate life
has made her his.

No wife, mine thought,
wived it enough,
if not distraught
and breaking stuff.

For all the snide
belittlement
yours used to hide
his self-contempt,

marriage to him
would soon disclose
the small boy in
a grown man's clothes.

Though mine thought I
could never be
unanguished by
my cuckoldry,

her strayings staled
with time, attrition,
the voids they veiled,
and repetition.

Granted, they were
suffering too:
I provoked her,
he failed at you.

Now, to all those
who think to judge us:
if this ode grows
acrid with grudges,

know that we weigh
the wrongs we bore
less than each day
we stayed for more.

From the twinned sources
of our joint grief,
matching divorces
brought us relief

by severing ties
we *sometimes* miss,
as butterflies
their chrysalis.

"Still Possessed of Those Effects"

Memory, that staid impresario,
prosceniums your past;
repertoried stagings,
a familiar cast.

On quaintness of sets and costumes
you smile from your box,
then wince suddenly, like a Claudius
when *The Mousetrap* locks.

Spotlit: *the very worst thing*
you've ever done—
a backstory you haven't told
anyone—

you never got caught—
nobody saw—
no one even talks about it
anymore—

(Setting aside that character
who may yet, of course,
uncage a long-starved revenge
on your bleating remorse.)

So here you sit, unpunished
to this very day,
hardly the sticky end scripted
for the villain you play.

Now what *would* be tragic, is dreading
some fifth-act brawl,
as if justice were poetic *after*
the curtains fall.

Unscripted

Jumbled with you in a five-AM embrace,
I lacked words to say, love, how I'd just dreamt
of coming home one night to find you dead,
and of grief then hunting me through a maze
of bleached-out, neverending nothingscapes;
but as light through parted curtains revealed
the impatient day outside, I prolonged my hold
as if to prove you mine and not the grave's.

Lovers long married seldom talk of death,
and if they do, only with an awkward air
suiting scenarios never run through before,
and this is wise: for how should they confess
waking to know themselves rehearsed to lose
the still-dreaming spouses they clasp so close?

Johnson Penitent

Uttoxeter-market, 1784

Slab-featured, stiff-limbed, blinking, fat,
    the old man lumbers through the stalls.
In one thick hand he grips his hat.
    On his limp wig the cold rain falls.

His guarded look in passing me
    warns that he knows I know his name,
the satirist of vanity
    mocked by the nemeses of fame.

Layabouts and curs, who presume
    to search out harm in what is odd,
swiftly converge on him, for whom
    their jeers are flicks from the lash of God.

The knife-stab laugh, the flaying stare
    wilt, when they dare him to his face;
on he goes, muttering with the air
    of one too proud to shirk disgrace.

Brusquely urbane, sagely uncouth,
    vulnerable and contemptuous,
he halts at last before a booth
    and turns, and scowls, and squints at us.

There for an hour, more or less,
    he stands, encircled and alone,
defiant in his wretchedness,
    more used to judge than to atone.

The sight soon draws only those few
    too drunk or mad to feel the rain;
not even the self-pilloried stay new
    for long. He left the way he came.

Good Sir, whatever drove you here,
    be it some debt of grief or pride,
be it folly, or be it fear,
    I would your need were not denied.

The Examined Life

I.

Of the uncleared Amazons yet within,
how prudent a steward has the poet been?
No more prodigal than settlers who slash
vast emerald tracts, for a vegetable patch.

2.

To the life-long Lent of children forgone,
what penitent's faith tempted him on?
Simply the fear that too feasted a heart
would shrink from the fasts that nourish his art.

3.

"Always the craft, never the career":
do his works buttress a boast so austere?
Only as bastions, shaped to bar out
marauding hordes of steppe-spawned doubt.

4.

To mock every clique, yet then to miss
member's privileges: who does this?
Who but an exile, dismayed to find
no more to Siberia than his own mind?

Poem in which the Word Truth Does Not Appear: An Art of Poetry

1: In
How armatures of fact bare themselves to us best
within brackets of *as if,* is a question the poem answers
by seeming not to. Like the inheritance stalking an heir,
it waits at a lessening distance for those recognitions
only impoverishment can sugar. Such is our entrance
to spaces all the stranger for our brief belonging there.

2: Through
At your breath's touch, it rides smooth and cool beneath
a first light gliding caress, then warm and muscled
when pressed, knobbed nodes, slick clefts, a luscious plunge
among velvet depths, a climb along strung cadences
of out-thrust and in-swerve: the ribs under the skin under the
      hand
of your voice. Tongue-flesh: stretched, slacked. Undulant.
      Enrapt.

The emerald pebbles and purple shells of its phrases
must tumble long in the waves' rough outrushing ebb
to flash like glass, polished, cracked, in the gargling crease
of surf aswirl with sand. Yours for the stooping,
rinsed, ranked amid shelf-silt and sill-scurf, they allude
to neons nowhere seen but in deep, ink-blue seas.

Traverse its tropes like streets through that Rome the real Romes
just imagine. Still-urgent murals emerge from crusts
of overpaint. Palaces cannily edit their unkempt splendor

to complement your mood. Spires blur on the oozing mirror
of a slate-blank river. Yet a certain mimosa-roofed square,
as if unrevisited, remains as remembered.

Threading a domed-over gloom's throng of fraught bronzes,
you sense its grandeur turn and scowl. With each step
through the ambient marble chill, a tomb-slab's text
looms semi-legible. Aloft, stiff-robed forms flex wings
in postures too ecstatic for irony to intercept
the weird, abrupt, all-altering wordlessness of awe.

Along its sightlines trained on the future, your view
snags on barbed knots of now, must rip from itself
what clings or else hang like script looped from punctures.
Page after wrongful page peels you a shame
unassuageably pure, since injustice, unseen as agreed,
thickly palimpsests every gilt fleck of fading text.

3: To
In bored-past-enduring exclusion from the paywalled given,
she reads. On guard against rain-sequined irises
peaking with routine facility, he reads. To tap
the naïveté that will nectar tongues caked numb
with traffic's lead tang, they must read. For the balm of absence
become snugly present, the whisper of things far

nestling near, the lift of fixtures loosed, we can read. In austere
solidarity with annalless thwarted anonyms, it's read now
or Lear out later. Of that human you were never to be
but are, read. Of those lost, as of those not, read,
and of readers too, re-entered on a brief beautiful
afflicting world, as much ours, as is, as other than it is.

Elsewhere Altogether

Like a walltop's fangs of glass, defunct casinos gleam
round our Great Inland Sea's waterless shore;
hazard-suited scavengers roam its ochre dunes
where indigene ruins pock in the alkali air.

In the distant South's permafrost wastes, the Rectified
are enduring the purge of cold. Pardon is rare.
By ancient custom, each newborn male receives
their macabre handicrafts of horn and fur.

Friezes show the Poet-Kings, dynasts of the Seed Age,
sternly wielding the wasp-stingered scourge of shame
against our still barbarous tribe. Though their line died out
and codices burned, superstition still blots their names.

Sheer alpine valleys and far East Gulf archipelagoes
shelter the austere remnants of the Old Creed.
None but priests can hymn its glyphs. Night roofs the haunted
      rites
of the long-hunted. Their least myths thrive like weeds.

Shrewd candidates know that, to this nation, wisdom sounds
like the bitter ramblings of mad billionaires;
justice, like the damp smack of meat on cement; and courage,
like garbled place-names from a dozen current wars.

Razor-wired ziggurats down our capital's boulevards
canalize the crunching melees of protest and police.
Embassies rise from slumlands. Floodlamps scrub fenced-off
      squares.
Old women swathe cenotaphs in heraldic wreaths.

One Tessera More

Savoring springlike winter weather,
wife and husband lounge together;
TV off, windows wide,
we are pleased to stay inside
upon the sofa, where you gaze
back at morning's level rays
and, serenely as arcs that sky,
part one from the other thigh.

Now first I glimpse your nether zone
lingeried in light alone;
no staid underclothes here eclipse
the full-on splendor of those lips,
where lissome sunbeams slantwise fling
silk's most gorgeous glistening
to splash, on each pleat and fold,
palest prelapsarian gold.

Yet alas! now that I possess
this vision of the sun's caress,
what mundane fabrics can replace
the sheer delights of solar lace?
When again will my eyes play
like Adam's on the world's sixth day?
Ah, must this zippered-up existence
muffle all such dazzling instants?

But for now, my love, let us seize
such gemlike chips of time as these,
and true them up to tessellate
the plaster walls and walks of slate
all our lost hours show, but those
where memory's mosaic glows:
woman and man, limned in glass,
their passions lustrous, as they pass.

Horace: *Carmina* I.9

Do you see how Mount Soracte shines with snow
against the sky, how its trees strain to bear
     their burden, how the river's flow
     stands motionless in the sharp air?

Come, my convivial friend, close out the cold,
and let the fireplace never want for wood;
     uncork that twenty-five-year-old
     single malt. Two fingers: that's good.

Forget all the rest, let what is to be
be: not long will this violent wind, that thrashes
     to a vaster violence our sea,
     trouble your cypresses and ashes.

As for tomorrow, take whatever chance
sends you, and count yourself ahead. Don't sneer,
     young man, should you be asked to dance,
     don't mock love's blisses out of fear,

while age has yet to whiten your hair and sour
your mind. Now, as night falls, the city squares
     belong to couples; now is the hour
     for low-voiced words, for love affairs,

and for a girl, whose hiding-place is found
by her sweet laugh, to wear her favorite charm
     no more, a prize snatched from around
     her half-struggling, half-proffered, arm.

Tu Quoque

As I scroll through the news feed, my inner Robespierre
curtly demands
the severed heads of all whose mulishness
hampers his plans.

Pedestalled Justice and pedimented Progress
join him, to urge
mass-dumpstering the unredeemables
in an overdue purge.

Reform? Please. While we're pimping our principles out
to compromise
and starving our passion in a cage of patience,
injustice thrives.

So keep your Solons and your Lincolns, I'm
in the mood for a Mao,
proof that true power means your wants get fulfilled
right fucking now.

Ending this long dark night of venal unreason
only *seems* complex:
as they say Lenin said, if you want the omelet,
you break the eggs.

By all means, let the act of closure be swift:
I am no sadist.
Compute each method's throughput rate—we'll use
whichever's greatest.

Think of their strident witless blather transformed
to a silence so huge
that it claims us a place in the rankings even higher
than the Khmer Rouge.

Since you're still reading, I must assume
you too keep a list
of those who can do this world no finer favor
than not to exist.

So an *obersturmführer*, a *génocidaire*,
and a commissar
(stop me if you've heard this) walk one evening
into a bar.

The place is packed. They sit. When the bartender asks
what it is they'll have,
the commissar says, "Shots—*for everyone!*"
I won't tell if you laugh.

White Man's Blues

Well I'm walking down the street,
        there's no English to be heard;
yeah, I'm walking down my street,
        ain't no English, not one word.
I was born in the First World;
        looks like I'll be buried in the Third.

First they take away your job,
        send the factory off to Mexico;
then they go after your woman;
        where she's got to, I ain't know;
now they're coming for what's left,
        time for another Alamo.

I hear them say *white man*
        with that look on they face;
everybody saying *white man*
        like it have some nasty taste;
seems like they forget
        who it is owns this place.

Our daddies had it good,
        everybody knew God was white;
our daddies kept it simple,
        you black if you not white;
if that means they done wrong,
        I got no use for doing right.

Prisons full and getting fuller,
        because the law is the law.
How come we got so many prisons?
        And who is it writes the law?
Ask too many questions,
        you find out what prison's for.

In New York they call me racist,
        mock my accent and my state;
to L.A. I'm just a redneck,
        love two things, guns and hate;
but I'm the first to get a call
        when there's a war that can't wait.

Had a dream last night:
        a river of strangers rushing by;
no one hears me or sees me,
        and then that flood, it runs dry.
I knew when I woke up
        nothing changes till I die.

Made New

In bed that night you talked of school,
   of the friends you'd had, prizes you'd won,
and of the poems you'd learned by rote
   under the regime of some long-dead nun.
Asked for a sample you paused, then gave me
   "The Beggar Maid" by Tennyson
To *In robe and crown the king stept down*,
   but could not go on as you'd begun.

Curious, I went and looked it up:
   not one of Alfred's best, I'm afraid.
Yet you read it out, smiling at its rhymes
   like once-loved playthings long mislaid,
while with every verse I hear your voice
   lighten to a singsong it last displayed
when you stood at your desk reciting such things
   in the quavery lilt of the seventh grade.

And before it ends, this cloying tale
   of silent women and sovereign men
serves, as no reminiscence could,
   to summon back the girl you were then:
guileless, winsome, poised to flee,
   yet artful enough, at the age of ten,
that poor things turn, at your touch, too precious
   for me ever to dare scoff at again.

Uncle Bob Tells a Joke

I.
Around a kitchen table, three men sit
    drinking and talking. A small boy looks on.
Downstairs, their mother lets *Gunsmoke* acquit
    her country of weakness in Vietnam.

Then Bob, youngest and dimmest of the three,
    stubs out his Lucky Strike, ringpulls a beer,
and leans in with a palm on either knee.
    His grin alerts them, *This you'll want to hear.*

First he pretends to check if they're alone.
    Half the fun is the accent and the face.
The punchline jackpots in a hearty tone
    that deftly leagues the four of them by race.

Hoarse guffaws. The wives know to keep away.
    From the hall, Grandma shouts *Quiet!* again.
Each minute past bedtime the boy can stay
    affirms his place up here among the men.

In bed at last, he broods over Bob's joke;
    uncles and fathers can't, he knows, be cruel.
So he was eager, soon as he awoke,
    to tell everyone—even *them*—at school.

2.
I saw those three less and less. Now they're dead.
   Living as though all we shared was a name,
which should have proved me different, proved instead
   refusal had contoured me just the same.

Like shears that scissor out a silhouette
   across what seems one sameness while together,
we clip the outlines of our temperament
   with every commonality we sever.

A Very Short Trip to a Very Dark Place

I

Past midnight they drive
       down a back road,
unpaved, unlit,
       towards nowhere they know.
Where the highbeams push,
       the woods divide,
then shoulder in close
       around and behind.
They've left their city
       cloaked in a blaze
that cottons its sky
       like breath on a pane,
for this least-peopled place
       in a thousand miles,
their blind on a starfield
       no wastelight will hide.
He parks in a clearing,
       she pockets her phone,
the engine stops humming,
       the dashboard dims down,
and night in that instant
       ambushes them
with the truth of what passes
       for darkness back home.

II

Where the simmering wake
       of the Milky Way floats,

a gold like San Marco's
	in a blue like Van Gogh's
limns without lightening
	the opaque uncolor
that joins their silhouettes;
	then a noise, and it's over.
That was close. . . Something's coming. . .
	They know that we're here!
"Spectacular." "It is."
	"So we'll go then?" "Sure."
He slews the car round,
	she maps a way back,
the tires spew gravel,
	thank god they'd got gas.
All down the highway
	it's aftermath and laughter,
regret-slash-relief
	they didn't stay longer,
but no words just yet
	for what they imagined
stalking through the light
	that illumines nothing.

Eye Condition

Lately, should I look
at the farthest skies
or a close-clutched book,
lint-flecks surf my eyes.

Called "muscae," they drift
in granular strings,
just the kind of gift
a fifth decade brings.

Yet, though both eyes are
with these blobs infected,
think it not bizarre
they go uncorrected.

Squinting through a dust
tear-ducts cannot rinse
teaches me to trust
sight's contaminants.

If some wordscape floats
for one moment true,
these amoebal motes
smother its view.

If horizons get
drabber for this blur,
well might I forget
what dreambait they were.

I'll see blots because
treatment would disguise
none of the world's flaws,
and all of the eyes'.

November, the Realist

Scrapped leaves, the orange the gold the crimson,
scratch along, clump, stop. Crumble. Rot.
Blow off where it all blows. Aaannd are gone.
Goes, too, the wide green tight green ends in,
frou-frou for debleaking (Ablur? Ablur)
stark stonescapes that never otherhow were.
Boughs, stripped (check); ground, scraped (check); skies,
      lowdowned
and spilt-milk scrimmed (check, check). Sight: skimmed.
On view, brushstroked in rust/bone/ash/coal
and signed "November, the Realist": behold
your merest *is*, minus your *not.*

(Baits?) Yeah. (Taken?) Yup: nothing-worse winter,
spring ah-worth-it-all, why-worry summer.
Worst, last week a hue staggered you: "Use—
you there, sarcasto!—for once *le juste*, 'glorious'."
Then this. Gray air, sheer, non-swag. Brutal.
Concrete and brick. (Phones down!) Asphalt and metal.
Trust such to stand when plant-plush dismantles.
Sure, it's just until. But until until,
be sombered. Attend, figure, to your ground—
once back-, now fore-; more lack, less more—
where *with* withs nothing, without *without.*

Elegy for the Scholar of Palmyra

I

Three pickups low with men and a black van
pull up at the museum—his museum—
near where groves of discapitaled columns stand.
Beyond, jumbled blocks flare in the low sun.
Sullen families, bidden once more to come
by a hoarse male loudspeakered voice, wait to witness
this latest specimen of holy justice.

Even the children gasp as the van's door
suddenly gapes and the old man, unshaven
and grimy, stumbles blinking into the glare.
Decades of rapport with tyrants cannot save him
from disbelieving what is about to happen.
He is forced to kneel. A sword fulfills its purpose.
Doors slam and engines rev. The crowd disperses.

All afternoon, the corpse sprawls in a dust
milled by the wind from temples once the care
of this, their world-famed archaeologist,
whom no one now looks at or dares walk near.
Those heeding the next morning's call to prayer
glimpse first a slung-up, blood-bibbed, manlike form,
then, at its feet, the head with its glasses on.

A placard dangling there details his crimes—
apostasy, heresy, and the rest—
but not his months in prison, nor his screams
while tortured for a treasure he never cached,
nor how, for every "idol" they film defaced,
a dozen more will be trafficked out for weapons.
Theirs is the purity of men whose foes are heaven's.

II

Though warned, he refused to leave
ruins he had tended so long,
as if mere expertise
could keep marauders from
old gods left defenseless,
or save, from ready buyers,
some yet-unplundered fragments
of the splendor once Palmyra's.

And some, who follow from home
as horrors like Syria's happen,
called on there to undergo
no worse than to imagine,
surprised themselves by grieving
for Khaled al-Asaad,
as stones once in his keeping
succumbed to a younger god.

III

Sir, was it hope that would not let you flee
as the trucks closed in, or did you know even then
that the grandeur on show would waken their need
to match the breakage without to that within?

A mere bystander to your fate, I must
intrude on you no further than to mourn
how, from a world that is wolf to its own past,
one more of its shepherds is, alas, now gone.

To a Young Man Seen Wearing a Bow Tie

Backlook: gullet-ribbon, really?
in gluey August subway smother's
worn-raw forenoon of a Wednesday?
We flush damp, lean limp, seep fever,
while you waft easy, coolsome twenty,
spruce-o and spry in bruise-blue blazer!

Throatfast hourglass fusspiece—pfft!
Such priss! What prim! So fogey-me-in!
Why then? Sinecured CV-bloat?
Nana-lunch in privilege-den?
Power-uncle flunkey-chat
re data-clots in cubicledom?

Pinkwhite paisley nice-kid neckbind—
Pure non-now! Blithing through tie-downs
behooves. Book 'then' for your then-time.
Olding suits only the old-growns;
Fifth-Ave stiff-stuffs fray gray inside.
Clothes (life too), young you, nonce-blaze once.

Advice to a Painter

Now that your sitter's pose is right,
her hat just so, her fur cuffs flared,
the drapery plumped to snag the light,
a canvas stretched and its ground prepared,
    at last you can begin
    touching the colors in.

From their prismic arc round your palette, hues
glisten like buttery lumps of glass.
Forget for now how pigment, whose use
is letting all light's wavelengths pass
    but the one its texture reflects,
    redeems what it rejects.

Forget as well the earth's magmal heat
and abyssal crush, the eons expended
in churning darkness, that once discrete
elements might buckle, be blended,
    and subtly crystallize,
    bared secrets dazzling our eyes.

Let others detect, in the pleasure they take
from vermillion, the perils of mercury;
let them deplore how lead-white, now opaque,
will someday tarnish irreparably,
    or that, with bone-black, you spread
    soots compounded from the dead.

So flood your brush boldly with green,
malachite pilfered from a Tsar's hoard;
load another with ultramarine,
lapis from mineshafts slaves once bored;
    for the yellow a third receives,
    cows starved on mango leaves.

Your work is to show why sunbeams caress
cracked plaster dusting a carpet's pile,
that brass ewer, this brocaded dress,
and the face of one young girl, whose smile
    can only here endure,
    impeccably impure.

El Cortito

Wielding this, the "short-handled hoe,"
took staying stooped over too low
to see the skies it swung below.

*Choosing our tools is not allowed
where standing up means standing out;
only a boss can walk unbowed.*

*Death ends the work, made ours at birth,
of crouching in heat and rain and dirt
to learn how much our backs are worth.*

In straggling ranks across each field,
hands black-callused and hands red-peeled
compelled the tight-clasped earth to yield.

Whole migrant families, dawn till night,
made the ground feel the hack and bite
that kept the hooked steel's blade-edge bright.

*You like cheap produce? Then don't complain.
It's how we keep this workforce tame.
Where they come from, they're used to pain.*

Look at this one, uncrimping his spine!
One day's wages will pay your fine.
"But señor" nothing. Get back in line.

Women and men who worked the land,
marching with some too bent to stand,
at last got *el cortito* banned.

Hard to imagine, living like them.
It was wrong, but that was then.
Good thing it can't happen again.

Just Supposing

Suppose some promised catastrophe you seldom succumb to
        imagining
has, just now, stopped still not happening.

Suppose that last stark threshold, the one they've said all along
        (OK but for real this time) we must never blunder beyond,
is already joining all those others we've left behind.

Suppose, were this a movie (which don't worry it won't be), this
        moment'd be that cut between
the taut close-up on a bright zero closing out the countdown
and a silent wide shot across the impact zone.

Suppose that whether this news leaves you resigned or frantic,
        complicit or confessed, distraught, defiant, or bitter,
does not (and not once did and now as it has turned out never
        will) matter.

Suppose the coming days will make our folly's (though that won't
        be the name they use for it) inheritors envious
of (and this should really tell you something) us.

Suppose venality plus inertia. Suppose we'll worry about it then,
        or we've made mistakes before.
Then suppose terror and remorse. Suppose the anguish of
        irredeemable loss. Suppose blame. Suppose despair.

You can also suppose (though I don't recommend it) how we just
          missed (so close!) some nicer, non-nemesis-ridden, future.
Now suppose, as a kind of relief though not really but whatever,
how there won't be time for all that once it (i.e. catastrophe) gets
          here.

Suppose at least we won't have to talk about it ever again. That's
          something.
Suppose they're all wrong. (Told you so!) But they're not all
          wrong.

And finally, yes finally, suppose (if you dare) what it'll feel like
          then
to know how they (meaning we) knew now that, even as their (our)
          last chance to prevent it (i.e. catastrophe) is *juuuust*
          about gone,
they (we) are too busy to do more than wait for someone to hurry
          up already and find a fucking solution,
entertaining them(our)selves meanwhile with enough post-
          apocalyptic bullshit (but isn't some of it pretty cool?) to
          obscure how they (we) will surely deserve the curses of
          every coming generation,
which will not, however, reverberate all that long
because of, you know, oblivion.

The Monastery of Our Lady of Exile, Trinidad

A Benedictine abbey stands
high over the Caroni plain;
beneath the Saint's adorant hands
traffic hurtles into Port of Spain.

Tourists drive up a road cut through
untended orchards, parking where
they picnic and enjoy the view
beside the stillness of stilled prayer.

Down somber whitewashed galleries
shut cells, inscribed with pious words,
look down on lush encircling trees
bejeweled with obstreperous birds.

Where the hill's green surge ebbs below
the overhanging belvedere,
a graveyard's weed-grown pathways show
that grief now summons no one here.

An aged, vast flamboyant tree,
spangled with tiers of vivid red,
drapes in its lacework canopy
this unregarded patch of dead.

Cut for each European name
are dates, lifespan, and place of birth,
mere hints of how its owner came
to lie in Trinidad's rich earth.

A French Mother Superior,
said to be meek, and loved by all;
a Welsh merchant, whose profits were
his answer to his Savior's call;

a missionary schooled in Rome;
a Dutch soldier; a German clerk;
all sailed here from their northern home
to die while doing an Empire's work.

From those they thought to civilize
these headstones now beg peace in vain,
as shopping malls and suburbs rise
out of plowed-under fields of cane.

Set apart, as they wished, by race,
the staid pretensions of these stones
will yet keep them from the disgrace
of daylight baring their rotting bones,

till something like oblivion
recalls how these forgotten graves
attest to all that once was done
for gold and sugar, souls and slaves,

and will descend on them at last
and on their age's epic crimes,
and, to the madness of the past,
deflect the eyes of future times.

Passing cars leave a place now older
and smaller than at first it seemed,
as those laid here obscurely molder
on, undisturbed and unredeemed:

a dozen minor functionaries,
whose place among the dispossessed
finds, in this least of cemeteries,
neglect enough to seem like rest.

Just Like That

Moments like this, the surround shifts.
Your inboxes blinking with dire matters
flutter like drapes, then fade to disclose
some rubbled aftermath where wailing mothers
slump on blood-washed hospital floors.

Or if, that day, the surround consists
of boulevards down which you amble,
your shadow dimming shoes and watches
asplay in plate-glass boutique windows,
with one deep blink it all peels away
and you sprawl, too filthy not to ignore,
camped under roaring off-ramp arches.

The surround can flicker out even at home:
sprawled on the sofa, four feet on the table,
as the lived-in colors click to grays
just like that, every humble thing
now hateful, hated, bluntly reminding
how you, once partnered, now lounge alone.

In the Tanneries

From a high rooftop terrace, tourists look down
on this cubist jumble of pits, its white-tiled grid
manholed by poppy-red and henna-brown,
saffron and lead-based black. A few workmen sit
chatting amid the miasma of pigeon shit
that wafts, even up here, an assaultive smell
which the mint-leaf nosegay you clutch cannot wholly dispel.

A natural source, says your guide, of ammonia, guano
scrubs goat-reek from hides and scours off their wool.
You nod. Makes sense. Yet you wonder why there are no
implements to plumb each opaque basinful
less precious than limbs. As you feel some scruple pull
your wakening outrage up short, the glass of tea
just served you tastes like a breach in solidarity.

Descending stairs plush with scrap-drifts, you stand
among the vats, and nod to a man hastening by
who bears, in either bleached and puckered hand,
thick sheaves of goatskins dripping deep green dye.
This is how 'hand-made' is made. And though you try
not to shrink too plainly away, you despise
the poorist you saw him see before you lowered your eyes.

Here the pelts dry. Yes. Here they are shaved smooth.
And here the drone of a treadled sewing machine
evokes an old-timey sweatshop air, as you move
about this otherwise Bosch-ready scene.
Tour's over. Further sights pall, pinched between
where, given what you are, you do not belong,
and what, given who you are, you cannot doubt is wrong.

Later, in a café, a strange boy joins
and charms you, riffing in the dozen languages
he has cadged from accosted travelers like coins,
until, asked what he will be, young Omar says
"In the tanneries," and that's it, for you, for Fès.
They've brought your check. You'll be in New York again
in a few days. Stick to monuments and museums till then.

Authority Figure

His words, waking me from the sleep of five,
mocked some small feat of mine others had praised,
as if I, even then, were too long alive
not to begrudge sweet things their aftertaste.

Ten years later, prohibitions on his tongue
could restrain me from nothing but restraint,
until one day, but not when I was young,
I knew myself by my waywardness tamed.

Such an ironist was I at twenty-one
that I drew, from the anguish with which he spoke
of the failure it seemed I must become,
merely the makings of another joke.

So it was I found my most constant guide
in a voice heard only to be defied.

Trash

Busy elsewhere, we did not see
when that plastic shopping bag
kited some vortex of debris
till its hand-holds looped a snag
here, atop this locust tree.

That was last fall. Day by day
leaves hoarded for the past year
flared, died, and were flung away;
trees once lush now rose severe
from strewn gold soon to decay.

But the trees' becoming lack
turned to spoliation when,
like a jellyfish, the sack
would bloat, sag, and bloat again,
sickly white against their black.

Ceaselessly, all winter long,
from a thrashing branch it strained,
flimsy, shapeless, yet so strong
that as spring passed, it remained
crackling through the blackbirds' song.

Summer swathes the locusts now
in leaflets so luminous,
so sun-plumbed, as to allow
even the least deceived of us
to forget what wrings that bough.

Tactics

All fathers die.
Some children grieve,
left wondering why
theirs had to leave.

Some dread to cross
conscience's ban,
suffering from loss
long as they can.

Some, who abet
what memory does,
briskly forget
the man he was.

Others forgive,
fearing the fate
of those who live
orphaned by hate.

Repine, recall,
retouch, release;
I have tried all,
and find no peace.

This Poetic Life

Nothing will ever match the freedom of these,
your first commitments, of necessity
made with a lack of craft that guarantees
they seem inspired: right, unimprovably.

With each fresh scheme, your choices disallow
every line of development but one,
this one, the merely not otherwise, now
barely attaining form before it's done.

A further threshold sets you wondering
how so selfless a love of conceit could,
with practice, unfit you for everything
but the acts of closure over which you brood.

Too soon, but now, arrives the abrupt sloughing
off of your last few variants. Then nothing.

The Stargazers

Late one night in Yucatán,
wandering through the banyan trees,
we soon found our pathway ran
far too dark for the eye that sees
by Sirius and Pleiades.

Starshine: a phenomenon
exotic to the urbanite,
for whom a sun is hardly gone
before phalanxed streetlamps light
the shorewash of encroaching night,

leaving us as brightly blind
as does daytime's blue-white scrim
to the engulfing black behind.
Earth's cocoon, now lit, now dim,
hides all voids but those within.

We knew ourselves far from home
as, with every nightlight out,
brilliants in the obsidian dome
blazed too heatlessly to doubt
voids on voids recede without.

Yet the absence filling that sky
taught how blink-like lifetimes are
all in vain, while you and I
basked in beams flung parsecs far
from each long-constellated star.

If I Forget Thee

Have you seen the Holy Land,
climbed up Zion Hill,
stood in line to kiss the shrine,
begged to know God's will?

Was it here the Temple stood?
Here, that Jesus fell?
Did Muhammad rise into the skies
this close to the Kotel?

Were Via Dolorosa's tourists
indifferent to your grief?
Did you riot or stay quiet
on the *Haram al-Sharif*?

When the sun blazed down on you
from the Rock's gilt Dome,
did you see there sanctity
or just its vanished home?

Who or what did you decide
decides what is whose—
scripture? scholars? soldiers? dollars?
last night's cable news?

Say a settler shoots a farmer,
an Arab stabs a Jew:
do you regard it very hard
to choose between the two?

Has your God made enemies?
Are you afraid they'll win?
Do you and yours fight only wars
in defense of Him?

Are those prayers that you repeat
a symptom, or a cure,
for what began when Abraham
pulled up stakes in Ur?

Suppose you answer me at last;
suppose my questions cease;
would you then, Jerusalem,
think the silence peace?

Nocturne

Off to the east, late evening dissolves
your intricate distances into the blue
of a long-gentled wake, cut there when dawn
candied these panes in its tangerine glow.

But along the skyline bristling behind you
where ambers converge on angled bronze,
daylight's spent tide is draining away
while a silent, starless indigo comes.

Notes

"The Death of Gaddafi": *Now just a poor, bare animal, soon to die*, cf. King Lear, III.iv.110

"Climbing Mount Royal": In 1535, French explorer Jacques Cartier was guided to the top of this small mountain by local Iroquoians. The epigraph quotes "Ruins of a Great House," from *In a Green Night: Poems 1948-1960.*

"The Road to Lake Avernus": Located not far from Naples, this volcanic lake appears in the works of Virgil and other classical writers as the entrance to the underworld; its name derives from a Greek word meaning "birdless," presumably referring to the effect, no longer observable, of its toxic fumes.

"A Change of Sky": Title & epigraph from *Epistles* I.11.27.

"At the Frick": Henry Clay Frick, coke magnate, erstwhile partner of Andrew Carnegie, and breaker-in-chief of the 1892 Homestead Strike, left his mansion and art collection to the City of New York upon his death in 1919. In the museum's Parlor, preserved as Frick left it, Holbein's *Sir Thomas More* and *Thomas Cromwell* flank El Greco's *Saint Jerome*; Bellini's *Saint Francis in the Desert* is hung nearby. Goya's *The Forge* is the museum's only painting depicting manual labor. Frick's last words refer to the Gospel of Mark, 4:25.

"In the Ruins of a Tyrant's Palace": The Roman Emperor Tiberius withdrew to his palace, known as the House of Jupiter, on the island of Capri in 26 CE and governed from there until his death some eleven years later.

"All Before Them": title from *Paradise Lost*, Book XII, l. 646

"Leaving the Anne Frank House": On July 15, 1944—only three weeks before her arrest—Anne Frank, then fifteen years old, wrote in her diary: "It's a wonder I haven't abandoned all my ideals, they seem so absurd and impractical. Yet I cling to them because I still believe, in spite of everything, that people are truly good at heart."

"Still Possessed of Those Effects": *Hamlet* III.iii, Claudius speaking:

> *My fault is past. But, O, what form of prayer*
> *Can serve my turn? 'Forgive me my foul murder'?*
> *That cannot be; since I am still possess'd*
> *Of those effects for which I did the murder,*
> *My crown, mine own ambition and my queen.*
> *May one be pardon'd and retain the offence?*

"Johnson Penitent": As a teenager, Samuel Johnson once refused to accompany his father, Michael, a bookseller, to work at Uttoxeter-market; later in life (fifty years to the day, if one early biographer is to be believed) he revisited the town and mortified himself in the manner the poem describes. The story can be found in Boswell's *Life of Johnson*, ed. Hill, rev. Powell: vol. IV, p. 373.

"Elegy for the Scholar of Palmyra": On August 18, 2015, Khaled al-Asaad, for over 40 years the chief archaeologist and custodian of the ancient Syrian city of Palmyra, was publicly beheaded by members of ISIS, and his mutilated corpse was displayed in the manner described.

"Advice to a Painter": Finally banned in 1890 after centuries of export from Bengal to Europe and elsewhere, 'Indian yellow' was a pigment concocted from the urine of cows fed only on the leaves of the mango tree.

"El Cortito": 'The short one,' a hoe so truncated it kept its user

continually bent over, was finally banned for use in California in
1975. Countless farm laborers, including United Farm Workers
leader Cesar Chavez, suffered permanent debility and chronic
pain after being required to work with it. Their stooped posture
made it easy for field bosses to detect even the shortest cessation
of labor.

"If I Forget Thee": Title from Psalm 137. 'Kotel' is the Hebrew
name for the Western Wall; 'Via Dolorosa,' or Street of Sorrow,
is the supposed route along which Christ carried the Cross;
'Haram al-Sharif,' or Noble Sanctuary, is the Arabic name for the
Temple Mount and the site today of the gilded Dome of the
Rock. 'Ur': Genesis 11:31.

Acknowledgements

I am very grateful to the editors of the following journals, in which these poems (or earlier versions of them) first appeared: *Acumen, Blue Mountain Review, Blue Unicorn, Cleaver Magazine, The Comstock Review, Crosswinds Poetry Journal, CutBank, Flyway: Journal of Writing and Environmen, f(r)iction, Front Range Review, Heirlock Magazine, Illuminations, Lucky Jefferson, The Lyric, The Midwest Quarterly, Mobius: The Journal of Social Change, New Ohio Review, The New Verse News, Orbis, Panoplyzine, POEM, Poetry Salzburg Review, Quiddity, The Raintown Review, The Road Not Taken, The Rotary Dial, Saranac Review, The South Carolina Review, The Sow's Ear Poetry Review, Talking River Review, Third Wednesday, THINK: A Journal of Poetry, Criticism, and Reviews, Toho Journal, Trinacria, typishly, Vallum, The Wisconsin Review,* and *Xavier Review.*

About Atmosphere Press

Atmosphere Press is an independent, full-service publisher for excellent books in all genres and for all audiences. Learn more about what we do at atmospherepress.com.

We encourage you to check out some of Atmosphere's latest poetry releases, which are available at Amazon.com and via order from your local bookstore:

The Stargazers, poetry by James McKee
The Pretend Life, poetry by Michelle Brooks
Minnesota and Other Poems, poetry by Daniel N. Nelson
Interviews from the Last Days, sci-fi poetry by Christina Loraine
the oneness of Reality, poetry by Brock Mehler
Drop Dead Red, poetry by Elizabeth Carmer
Aging Without Grace, poetry by Sandra Fox Murphy
No Home Like a Raft, poetry by Martin Jon Porter
Mere Being, poetry by Barry D. Amis
They are Almost Invisible, poetry by Elizabeth Carmer
Auroras over Acadia, poetry by Paul Liebow
Transcendence, poetry and images by Vincent Bahar Towliat
Adrift, poetry by Kristy Peloquin
Time Do Not Stop, poetry by William Guest
Ghost Sentence, poetry by Mary Flanagan
What Outlives Us, poetry by Larry Levy
What I Cannot Abandon, poetry by William Guest
All the Dead Are Holy, poetry by Larry Levy
Who Are We: Man and Cosmology, poetry by William Guest

About the Author

A New Yorker by birth and likely by death, James McKee enjoys failing at his dogged attempts to keep pace with the unrelenting cultural onslaught of late-imperial Gotham. His studies in English & Philosophy at the University of Virginia instilled in him a love for artful language and a corollary desire to escape academia forever. He subsequently held a number of ludicrously unsuitable jobs before spending over a decade as a teacher and administrator at a small special-needs high school, no doubt learning valuable lessons thereby about the ironies of fate. Of the two paradigms of writerly effort—Keats, whose writing came "as naturally as leaves to a tree," and Thomas Mann, who defined a writer as "someone for whom writing is more difficult than it is for other people"—McKee knows he belongs to the latter but hopes to awaken one day a member of the former. He currently works as a private tutor and lives with his wife in the Borough of Queens, which is or should be the destined epicenter of American cultural rebirth. He spends his free time, when not writing or reading, traveling less than he would like and brooding more than he can help.